PLAYING
Small

The Actor's Guide
To Becoming
A Booking Magnet

CHRISTINE HORN

Playing Small: The Actor's Guide To Becoming A Booking Magnet

Copyright © 2019 by Christine Horn

Chocolate Superstar Publishing
PO Box 4234
Chatsworth, CA 91313
hello@whyplaysmall.com
www.whyplaysmall.com
www.christinehorn.com

Paperback ISBN: 978-1-7339812-0-0
Ebook: ISBN: 978-1-7339812-1-7

Library of Congress Control Number: 2019939805

Cover Photography by: B. Alyssa Trofort
Makeup, Hair & Styling by: Day Byrd
Edited by: Flora Brown
Cover photo wardrobe courtesy of: Janice Roye (Wardrobe Stylist @vintage751)
Book cover and interior design: Grzegorz Japoł (book-cover.design)

Printed in the United States of America.

Any references to historical events, real people, or real places are used fictitiously. Names, characters, and places are products of the author's imagination.

Chocolate Superstar Publishing books may be purchased for educational, business, or sales promotional use. For information, please email: sales@whyplaysmall.com

Praise for **Playing Small**

"Christine Horn is an extraordinary actress and a focused career coach for actors! This book displays her innovative approach to a career in entertainment and is pitch perfect for every actor of every age from the millennial to the empty nester. Don't hesitate, read this book to be on your way to becoming a booking magnet!"

— Saycon Sengbloh,
Tony® Award nominated Actress and host of SayconTalks
www.saycontalks.com

"Christine's book is absolutely spot-on. Her message of facing your fears, empowerment and self-love is essential to success in today's industry. Please don't settle for just reading this book. Do what it says, and see what a difference it will make in your acting career."

— Dallas Travers,
Award Winning Author of The Tao of Show Business

"I couldn't put this page turner down. At the end, I thought, where was Christine when I was coming? Desperate to get to the next level of my career…thinking there was something wrong with me because I kept hearing the word "No." Retreating back to my shell to lick my wounds…nothing was wrong with me. I was just playing small! On behalf of all the actors getting ready to read this – THANK YOU CHRISTINE."

— DaJuan Johnson,
Emmy® Nominated Actor and Founder of Think Bigger Coaching
www.thinkbiggercoaching.com

"I love how Christine's book encourages your undefeatable spirit to recognize the power of being scared and doing it anyway. She lets you see that you are not alone in feeling small, to the point where it actually levels the playing-field and becomes inconsequential. She gives you tools to learn to distance yourself from that "wicked little negative voice" in your head, and instead embarrass the wondrous possibilities of being the artist you were born to be."

— Crystal Carson,
Los Angeles Acting Coach and Owner of Auditioning by Heart Studio
www.crystalcarson.com

*"Greatness is inevitable
when focus marries passion
and the desire is just as strong as the need."*

- Freddie Hendricks

Dedication

This book is dedicated
to every Hollywood Bound Actor with a dream.

I see your heart.

I feel your fears.

I share your vision.

This book was inspired by you.

This book was written for YOU.

Table of Contents

Acknowledgments

To my husband, Garland, for putting up with my long hours, late night self-tapes, diva attitude, and for leaving everyone you know to move across the country with me so that I could live my dreams. I am eternally grateful for your loyalty and support.

To Saycon, for all the video chats, tears, and encouragement. Thank you.

To Day, for always giving me your ALL, whether it's in friendship or business...thank you.

To Kail, for still managing to speak life into me, even if it was hard to do it for yourself. I love you.

To Freddie, for seeing greatness within me as I walked the halls of Tri-Cities High School. Because of you, I have the LOVE blueprint, and I get to share it with my students. Thank you.

Mom, I would need another book to share my gratitude for you. Thank you for ALWAYS supporting my vision and helping me every step of the way.

Dad, Christopher, Christel, Marisha, Sharalle... thank you for supporting me even when I'm far away and out of touch.

To my entire family, extended family and friends, thank you for loving me.

To every actor I've ever coached, Hollywood Bound Actor, YouTube, Instagram or Facebook viewer, I may not know all of your names, but I certainly feel all of your love. I'm humbled and honored that you've chosen me to come on your journey. I don't take that for granted. I believe in you. Thank you for believing in me.

Before we get started...

ONE: Join The Hollywood Bound Actors family!

I want you to know that I'm here for you. You are going to feel a lot of emotions as you read this book, and I don't want you to feel alone. I've created an amazing online community called Hollywood Bound Actors, and I want you to join us. We are a global collective of actors who are on a mission to elevate our careers and our lives. We relate to each other, and we uplift each other.

Our website: **www.hollywoodboundactors.com**

Join our Facebook group:

https://www.facebook.com/groups/hollywoodboundactors

TWO: Grab your FREE Get Booked! Playbook

I don't want you to read this book and then do nothing. I want to help you take action. I've created the **Get Booked! Playbook** and I want you to download it. I've put together an exclusive workbook and video training series to help you dig deeper with everything covered in this book. It's my gift to you.

Go ahead and grab your free copy at

www.whyplaysmall.com/workbook right now.

Ok.... NOW we can continue!

Introduction

You don't want to read this book. Seriously. I know you. You just want strategy.

"Tell me how to find better representation."

"Tell me how to find more auditions."

"Tell me how to book more gigs."

"Tell me how to win an Emmy® or an Oscar®."

I know you.

You already have strategy coming out of your ears. I'm not here to add to the noise that is already swirling around in your head.

Strategy isn't the reason you haven't been booking the way you want to.

You're avoiding the real reason:
Your thoughts are sabotaging your career.

You've made it. You are finally here. You have reached the point in your acting career where you've realized, this shit is hard. No one prepared you for this. You saw the red carpet and the glitz and glamour on television. You've been watching all the award shows since you were a child. You promised yourself that one day you too would stand on that stage.

You believed this would happen even when no one else did. Now you're here. You are still waiting on your BIG break and trying to stay hopeful and driven. Through the tears, lonely nights, frustration and all the emotional roller coasters, you're still here hanging on... barely. I want to welcome you to your next level.

You may already be thinking, Christine Horn is a nut if she thinks that THIS moment right here, right now is MY next level.

Just bear with me and let me explain.

I've been where you are. I know how it feels to be stuck between unknown and almost famous. I know how it feels to be surrounded by so many people yet feel so alone. Isolated. I know how it feels to be on the cusp of breaking through, but then a project doesn't pan out. I know about the financial woes that come with this life; the sacrifice of love, family, time, and travel. I know how it feels to be tired, frustrated and on the brink of throwing in the towel. I get it. I've been there and managed to not only break through this moment, but to soar into MY next level. So when I welcome you to your next level, I mean it with all sincerity.

This book was written for you. Yes, you.

I know you love what you do. So do I. I've been there. I want you to rest assured that you are right where you need to be — at this moment reading this paragraph.

Breathe. *(Seriously.)* Take a deep breath and allow me to share my story with you.

My Story

I began acting when I was a child growing up in Bronx, New York. I used to enter storytelling contests in elementary school. The first school play I performed in was "Cinderella and the Prince of Pollution" in the 5th grade. That was the play that let me know I was a pretty good actor and singer.

I took dance classes for years at Mind-Builders Creative Arts Center. I studied tap, jazz, ballet, modern dance... the whole shebang. My mother, Valerie, would take me to see on/off Broadway shows all the time. The first play that stuck out in my mind was "Mama, I Want To Sing."

Performing was all that I knew and all that I wanted to do with my life.

We moved to Atlanta, GA during the summer of 1992 and I enrolled in the Tri-Cities High School Magnet Program. This school changed my life. This is where I met my mentor and acting coach, Freddie Hendricks.

Outside of school, he also ran a youth theatre company called

The Freddie Hendricks Youth Ensemble of Atlanta. This theatre company changed not only my life, but also the lives of hundreds of young people around the globe (including some very famous people.) I spent years honing my craft and traveling with this troupe until I left to go back to New York to attend the American Musical Dramatic Academy. I only stayed one of the two years and left early to start performing professionally.

Like many actors, I held many jobs. Ask any friend of mine, and they will tell you that I am a woman who is NOT afraid of hard work. Maybe it's because I'm just a driven Sagittarius or because I've got Jamaican blood flowing through my veins, but I like to work. I like to meet goals. I like to pay my bills on time, and the greedy girl inside of me likes to be fed often.

I was blessed to work for the Bobby Dodd Institute in Atlanta on and off for over 15 years. They are a non-profit organization that helps people with disabilities become empowered and to find jobs. I would work there during the day and usually head to my night job waitressing for an awesome chef, Shaun Doty.

I always tell actors that there is absolutely NO SHAME in working 2 or 3 jobs to provide for yourself and your career. However, it's imperative that you find work that won't prevent you from doing the thing you say you want to do. I've always had full disclosure with my jobs about where my loyalties were. My acting career always came first. So that meant my manager was mad at me some days. The key to making this kind of relationship work is to have an amazing work ethic, be a self-starter, and bring so much value to your position (no matter what it is) that you become irreplaceable in your supervisor's eyes; that's what I did with all of my jobs.

My "big break" came in July 2006 when I got the call to join the national touring company of Disney's "The Lion King." This gig was life-changing. I ended up staying with the show for about 5 years, and by the end of my time in 2011, I had traveled with both touring companies, performed on Broadway, in Las Vegas, and even got to workshop the role of Nala in Hamburg, Germany. What a ride!

When the Las Vegas company closed, I decided that I was not going to go back to Atlanta. I found a room to rent in Los Angeles and drove there from Mandalay Bay Casino after the show closed.

I was ready to take Hollywood by storm!!!

I assumed that because I had Broadway credits and a few bit parts in some feature films that I would have no trouble finding an agent and booking my first series regular role. Boy, was I wrong!

What I didn't know at the time (and maybe you aren't aware either) is that television credits rule this industry. That's what it felt like. It was the ultimate catch 22. Do you want to act on television? Great! Just get some television credits first! Wait... what?

Now an unemployed actor living off savings and unemployment,

I managed to spend my days sending out mass mailings to random agents and managers in hopes of getting signed. I submitted on the Actor's Access website daily and landed some theatre roles and indie films and web series.

I eventually landed a commercial agent, a theatrical agent who NEVER called me, and a manager who did her best with what I had to offer.

I'm not going to lie. It got tough. Though I started to break ground within the Los Angeles theatre community, the salary was not enough to sustain my lifestyle.

My finances were dwindling, my health was suffering, and my mother was having some health complications due to her battle with Lupus. I was stressed, overwhelmed, in a long distance relationship that was strained, and I was behind on my mortgages for the property I owned in Atlanta. Something had to change.

I made a quick decision one day to move back to Atlanta once I realized that I was going to have to get a day job again. I figured if I was going to have to work a 9-5 and miss auditions (that I was not getting by the way), then I might as well do that around family and friends.

I called my old job at Bobby Dodd Institute and went back in 2012 just in time to help them train new staff.

To answer the question in your head... YES. I felt embarrassed, ashamed, like a failure, like just another actress who Los Angeles chewed up and spat out.

For a moment.

I filed bankruptcy to clear my debt and got my life back in order.

I vowed that I would one day go back to Los Angeles, but next time I would do it with a resume worth its salt and with a plan.

I went on a journey of self-exploration. I read every book I could get my hands on that is related to personal development, spirituality, self-help, and acting. I got in on-camera acting classes and hired a private acting coach for auditions (shout out to Vince Pisani for all of his guidance.) I knew I was meant for more. I just had to tap into the more that existed within me. More on that later.

Armed with new confidence and clarity, I became a booking magnet. That's a term I coined for myself. You will learn more about that in the coming chapters. I set a goal to take almost any role offered to me. I learned how to market myself to industry professionals. I learned how to perform on camera by watching everyone on set. I studied television like it was my night job. I knew that if I wanted to master something, I needed to study and dissect it.

In a couple of years, I racked up a bunch of co-star credits on network television shows, feature films, and got an amazing opportunity when I booked the recurring guest star role of Sherry Perkins on the USA network medical thriller, "Complications."

Though we only lasted one season, I was in 8 out of the 10 episodes that aired. I wanted to make the most of this attention, so I hired a publicist who ended up connecting me to a manager in Los Angeles who was willing to work with me long distance (which is rare.)

My relationship with my managers grew stronger when I booked a series regular role in a comedy pilot for ABC in 2016. Though it did not get picked up, my team saw potential in me and urged me to consider moving back to Los Angeles now that my credits were recognizable.

In February 2017, I convinced my husband Garland to take the journey with me to the west coast to give Los Angeles another shot. I felt it in my spirit that I was finally ready to "make it" in Hollywood. I also felt that I was reaching a ceiling in Atlanta. I wanted to be the star of the shows that came to film in our great city, not just a co-star.

It was a challenge to leave our friends and family behind, but we arrived in Los Angeles on Super Bowl Sunday, 2017. It was me, Garland, our dog Prince, and our box turtle, Superstar, ready to let Hollywood have it!

I quickly signed with theatrical representation and connected with my previous commercial agent. I booked my first network guest starring role my 3rd week back, and by March, I booked a recurring role in Ryan Murphy's Emmy® award-winning American Crime Story about the assassination of Gianni Versace!

Talk about confirmation.

The rest is history. I soon created the Hollywood Bound Actors online community as a way to coach new and experienced actors on all the things I was clueless about back in 2011. I wish I had the coach that I am to my clients — someone to share the REAL deal about how Hollywood works.

As you read through these pages, you will discover that my career changed when my mindset changed.

When I walk into an audition now, my confidence walks in the room before I do. I'm grounded with a strong sense of self. I know my worth. I know how talented I am. No one can take that away or deny that fact.

I've left desperation on the shelf. It does not exist within me.

It took time to get here.

In the coming pages, I will guide you on how to get there for yourself. It will change your career and your life.

I'm going to teach you how to STOP playing small and become a booking magnet.

Are you ready?

Part One
FACE YOUR FEARS

When actors first reach out to me for coaching, they usually start our first conversation telling me that they need more auditions. They want a magic pill that will instantly help them book more and become a casting favorite. They will often rattle off a list of things they are doing daily that have proven to be fruitless.

Once they are done talking, I ask one challenging question.

What are you afraid of?

This question usually takes the actor off guard. They are saying to themselves, *"Why is Christine asking me this? I need a strategy. Tools. Tell me how you are booking so much. I want to work a lot like YOU, Christine!"*

This question is so challenging because it forces you to look within, get honest and dig deep. This is where the work begins. Clarity is on the other side of this answer.

So, I am going to ask you the same question before you read any further.

What are YOU afraid of?

I have found in my own experience that WE actors suffer from 7 major FEARS. These fears range from no big deal... to paralyzing.

These 7 FEARS are the real reason you have not been booking the way you desire.

I will expound on each one in the pages to follow, but for now, scan the list to see if you can spot your personal weak spot:

Fear of Failure

Fear of Judgment

Fear of Success

Fear of Not Being Good Enough

Fear of Competition

Fear of Not Having Enough

Fear of Time Running Out

Can you relate to any of these?

Fear of Failure

"Failure is an event, never a person; an attitude, not an outcome; a temporary inconvenience; a stepping stone. Our response to it determines just how helpful it can be."

— *Zig Ziglar*

I know you want so many amazing things for your life. You have big dreams and desires. Your dreams for your career are so big and scary that they keep you up at night. Even when you try to quit this industry, your calling keeps calling you back. It's like a baby that is determined to be birthed. The dream sits in the pit of your stomach and nags at you no matter how much you try to ignore or bury it.

This is your purpose. You would not have been given this desire if the answer was not already created. You will come out on the other side. You will get the opportunity to experience your desires IF you don't quit. How? No one knows. You have to keep showing up for your dreams, and eventually, you will see the fruit of your labor.

There's only one problem. It's scary as hell to keep showing up for a dream you are not experiencing right now. It's even scarier to admit that you want this massive dream. So what do you do? You stay still. You stay stuck. You do nothing to move you towards your desires. You make excuses for why it won't work. You self-sabotage any opportunity to grow beyond your comfort zone. You don't fully prepare for your auditions. You don't work on your craft. You listen to nay-sayers and dream snatchers who know nothing about the entertainment industry. You allow yourself to play small and pretend you don't really want this, when in fact you do.

Why would you do such a crazy thing?

You are afraid to FAIL.

See, fear of the unknown is a dream killer. None of us knows what tomorrow will bring. It's hard to have faith in the unseen when the world tells us how hard it is to make it. You begin to doubt yourself, your talents, and your tenacity.

You wonder, *"Am I really cut out for this?"*

What I want you to understand right now is that failure is an event, NOT a person.

What does this mean?

It means that you may try something and it doesn't work out perfectly. You may have auditions that don't go as well as you hoped. You may write a film, and the script may not be all that great.

Trying is part of the process. When things don't work out in the way you hoped or if they don't get you the optimal result you desired, you are supposed to learn from that experience!

Embrace failing. It means you actually tried to do something.

How can you know what to do the next time if you never try to begin?

If all you do is speculate the worst case scenario, you will be left with nothing.

I've failed at so many things in my life; business opportunities, relationships, auditions, workshops, short films, albums, public speaking... you name it!

Guess what? I show back up and get better and better.

The only reason you are even reading this book right now is because I decided to show back up for myself and for YOU.

My first book, *"90 Days to DIVA: Daily Motivation & Mentorship To Help You Reach Your Goals"* was not perfect, but it's done.

How about you make a promise to keep showing up for your dream daily? Just promise yourself to do something for your acting career every single day even if it's only for 10 minutes.

Imagine how that consistency would impact your career.

If your dreams don't scare you, then they are not big enough.

I'm scared of my dreams every damn day. That's how I know that I am on target. My dreams feel like epic mountains I have to climb! I choose to take one step at a time with unwavering faith that I can achieve them. I usually don't know HOW they will come to fruition. That is not my job. That is for the universe to take care of.

Decide today that you will "play scared." Embrace the fact that fear is coming along for the ride whether you want it to or not.

In part 2 of this book, I will teach you how to deal with your inner critic when it shows up.

For now, say this aloud: **I AM GOING TO PLAY SCARED.**

Fear of Judgment

"What will people think?"

That one question is what has kept you from going full out towards your dreams of being an actor who works consistently.

You worry so much about what people will say if you:

Promote your upcoming bookings and gigs.

Create your own web series or short film.

Perform in a local play.

Use unorthodox marketing strategies to connect to industry professionals.

How many times have you talked yourself out of your greatness in fear of what someone else might think? Probably more times than you care to admit.

I am reminded of a famous quote from Theodore Roosevelt who says it best:

"It is not the critic who counts; not the man who points out how the strong man stumbles, or where the doer of deeds could have done them better. The credit belongs to the man who is actually in the arena, whose face is marred by dust and sweat and blood; who strives valiantly; who errs, who comes short again and again, because there is no effort without error and shortcoming; but who does actually strive to do the deeds; who knows great enthusiasms, the great devotions; who spends himself in a worthy cause; who at the best knows in the end the triumph of high achievement, and who at the worst, if he fails, at least fails while daring greatly, so that his place shall never be with those cold and timid souls who neither know victory nor defeat."

— *Theodore Roosevelt*

I'm going to let you in on a little secret.

You are being judged right now. Someone somewhere is judging you right now while you are minding your business reading this book.

You have done nothing wrong. You're not bothering anyone intentionally. You are just living your best life, trying to take your acting career to the next level, and someone is judging you. Isn't that freeing?!

Judging is part of human nature. We can't avoid it. People are going to think what they want to think about you because they can't help it. We ALL judge everything on a daily basis. We have all been blessed with individuality and strong opinions about what we like to eat, wear, relationships, and what we choose to watch on television.

You, my dear, have signed on to be an ACTOR. Our job is to perform and get judged on a daily basis. Every audition, every performance, and every photo you take... has to get judged for you to get chosen to do more of the work you love.

Once you accept that there is no way around being judged, you will begin to feel like a free-thinking individual. Make your choices in accordance with what YOU desire. It's already a challenge getting past your personal fears. If you add on the fear of judgment from strangers, your life and your career will never reach its true potential. I also want to be clear that many times, you fear the judgment of someone who is not even an actor! Someone who has never walked a mile in your shoes cannot tell you a single, solitary thing about the choices to make as an actor. Period!

Even people whose opinions you respect and value need to be taken with a grain of salt. Now, I'm not saying you should be arrogant and not listen to anyone or take advice. I am saying that you need to guard yourself against the opinions of the world.

I want you to get used to this now before you become famous. Celebrities deal with this at an abnormal level because they are household names. We (you and I) judge celebrities all the time. It's hard for them. It's hard for me. It's hard for you. We are all the same.

You don't get extra points for playing small.

The more you shine in your acting career and in your life you are naturally going to have more things to judge. You will be front and center in more people's lives. If they don't like it, or don't like you, they will have to get over it.

If you are going to be judged no matter what, why not go ALL out?

I will share one of my own quotes with you that you are welcome to steal,

> "Give all of your haters popcorn and tell them to keep enjoying the show."

> — *Christine Horn*

Fear of Success

When I coach actors in my Booking Magnet Academy about how to use my ninja strategies to book more work and build industry contacts, I get two types of responses, *"Exciting! This will take me to my next level. I'm doing this ASAP."* or *"Whoa. That sounds like a good idea and all, but that scares the crap out of me. Going that full out might actually get me the win I've been praying for, and to be totally honest, I'm not ready for that."*

Fear of success is very interesting because it is the close cousin to fear of failure. The way it differs is in how it shows up. With fear of failure, you are too scared to do ANYTHING. It's paralyzing. With fear of success; however, you say you want to achieve greatness, but your actions are always in contrast. It shows up as procrastination, self-sabotage, not following through, and extreme negative self-talk. You get stuck in a repetitive cycle of hoping and wishing and thinking your dreams and goals will manifest themselves *"someday."* We all know that *"someday"* is not on the calendar.

It takes courage to admit to the world and yourself that you actually desire to be a successful working actor. The idea of being an award-winning actor only seems far-fetched because that is where you have placed that thought in your mind.

It's easier to keep that dream as a faraway fantasy because then it never has to become real. When you make your goals and dreams public, you now have a responsibility to excel. As you begin to book more and more gigs, there will be an expectation of you as an actor to continue to deliver for each gig. The stakes only get higher. The roles only get bigger. You begin to wonder if you are really cut out for that type of pressure. Will you crack under pressure or will you thrive?

I can't tell you how many times I've been coaching an actor in one of my VIP programs and they spend months telling me how they want to book a recurring role on television. Together we train and craft a marketing plan to get on the radar of powerful casting directors. The day finally comes when a 10-page self-tape audition pops up. This should be good news. Instead, it turns into a panic fest. The actor starts to doubt their ability to deliver on everything they've been prepping for. Self-sabotage creeps in, they don't get coaching, and they end up either delivering a poorly prepped audition or they don't even submit it at all. Why? It's more comfortable to play small. It's more comfortable to stick to small co-star roles and stay under the radar.

Another reason some actors have a fear of success is because they fear what will happen after they *"make it."* Will there be pressure from family and friends to loan them money? *Will I lose friends because I'm famous? Will people think that I've changed? What if I book a big gig and then never work again? Will everyone think I'm a failure? What if I get typecast and stuck in a certain type of role? What if my boyfriend resents me? What if my children suffer from all the attention?*

What if, what if, what if. Do you see the downward spiral this can take?

Right now, I want you to permit yourself to shine. Give yourself permission to fully show up for your career and give it a real shot. Imagine what could happen if you fully committed to your career, acting classes, marketing, auditioning, and studying.

I want you to be playing the WHAT IF game with a positive spin. The way to do this is to take the negative thoughts you have about succeeding and turn them around.

Below are a few examples. Feel free to add as many as you need for your own situation.

Negative: What if my acting sucks?
Positive: What if everyone loved my performances and I became a highly sought after, award-winning actor?

Negative: What if I lose my close friends because I'm so busy and successful?
Positive: What if I become so busy and successful as an actor that my closest friends get to travel with me to filming locations and we take fancy vacations together?

Negative: What if my family and friends start begging me for money all the time and they get mad if I say "No?"

Positive: What if I start making so much money in my acting career that I was able to joyfully help my family and friends when they are in need and because of our close relationship they also understand and respect my boundaries?

Negative: What if people reject me?

Positive: What if I am loved and respected beyond my wildest dreams and I attract the people into my life who are positive, peaceful and only want the best for me?

Ok, now YOU try. Now is the time to become aware of your thoughts so that they do not control you. You control them. When a negative thought pops up, find a way to flip it into a positive, helpful thought. This will become easier as you do it more often.

Marianne Williamson's famous quote from her book *"A Return to Love"* is the perfect way to end this section.

> "Our deepest fear is not that we are inadequate. Our deepest fear is that we are powerful beyond measure. It is our light, not our darkness that most frightens us. We ask ourselves, 'Who am I to be brilliant, gorgeous, talented, fabulous?' Actually, who are you not to be? You are a child of God. Your playing small does not serve the world. There is nothing enlightened about shrinking so that other people won't feel insecure around you. We are all meant to shine, as children do. We were born to make manifest the glory of God that is within us. It's not

just in some of us; it's in everyone. And as we let our own light shine, we unconsciously give other people permission to do the same. As we are liberated from our own fear, our presence automatically liberates others."

— *Marianne Williamson*

A Return to Love: Reflections on the Principles of "A Course in Miracles"

Fear of Not Being Good Enough

We all want to be liked and accepted. It's human nature. When we decide to pursue an acting career for real, it can bring out all of our insecurities.

You think you have what it takes. Your friends tell you that you are a talented actor. Your parents are your #1 fans. Yet and still, you can't help but wonder if you actually have what it takes to make it.

Am I good enough?

The fear of not being good enough is a hard one to face because, in truth, not everyone is cut out for this business.

We've all heard that some people just have that "IT FACTOR." No one can ever tell you exactly what "IT" is... they just know it when they see it.

It's true, some people are naturally talented and born with a gift of acting. Then there are some of us who have a desire and need to constantly stay in class to even break ground as a beginner.

This is true in life no matter what line of work we choose to pursue.

We can't all be great at everything, but we can try.

To become a booking magnet, you owe it to yourself to see what you are made of. Accepting that you may not be the best is step one. Embrace where you are now. My acting abilities have grown tremendously over the last 20 years because I never quit. I stayed in class, performed in shows, took private coaching, and I stayed hungry.

Where you are today is not where you will be in 5, 10 or 20 years. Too many times as actors, we are so hard on ourselves and stuck in a cycle of comparison. It's okay to admire the performances of other actors, but don't let their talent dim the light on your own. Continue to be inspired by others and try and learn from them.

The only way to find out if you are good enough is to put yourself out there! Audition, audition, and audition some more. That is one of the main requirements of our job. With each audition, you will get better. Each time you get to act on camera or stage, you will get better.

Trust that where you are now is not where you will always be. Use your imagination to visualize yourself as a working actor who wows every audience that is blessed to experience you. Hold steadfast to that vision until it becomes your reality.

If you don't have an acting coach, get one. If you don't have a career coach, get one. If you have issues with your accent or speech, get a dialect/speech coach. There are so many resources available to you!

As actors, we always have to invest in our careers. It never ends. Whether we are spending money on headshots, costumes, makeup, hair, casting websites or coaching, it is understood that this is just par for the course.

You are expected to grow and blossom the longer you are on this journey. Now the choice is yours. Will you allow yourself to audition over and over again even if you don't see a booking for a while? Will you allow yourself to receive feedback that is helpful and essential for your growth as an actor?

If so, then you are one step closer to getting over the fear of not being good enough.

Remember this: There will ALWAYS be someone smarter, more attractive, and more talented than you. Accept that. The key is how you work with what YOU'VE got.

Actor, Will Smith, says it best...

> "The only thing that I see that is distinctly different about me is I'm not afraid to die on a treadmill. I will not be out-worked, period. You might have more talent than me, you might be smarter than me, you might be sexier than me, you might be all of those things you got it on me in nine categories. But if we get on the treadmill together, there's two things: You're getting off first, or I'm going to die. It's really that simple, right?

You're not going to out-work me. It's such a simple, basic concept. The guy who is willing to hustle the most is going to be the guy that just gets that loose ball. The majority of people who aren't getting the places they want or aren't achieving the things that they want in this business is strictly based on hustle. It's strictly based on being out-worked; it's strictly based on missing crucial opportunities. I say all the time if you stay ready, you ain't gotta get ready."

— *Will Smith*

Fear of Competition

You're not going to book every role you audition for. Period! No one does. Not even your favorite celebrity actors.

Now that we've established that, can we move on to the real lesson?

Are you ready? Here it is....

Stop worrying about everyone else. Your only competition is YOU.

I know what you're thinking, *"That's not true Christine. There are tons of actors who look just like me. We're the same type, and if there are so many, how will I stand out and book work?"* Would you like some cheese to go with your whine?

When I was just starting out in film and television, I would study the other local actors who I saw booked a lot. I spent so much time trying to figure out what they were doing and how they were doing it. I would Google them and try to put pieces to the puzzle that I created in my mind. You would have thought that

I had a job as a private investigator the way I was putting clues together.

Then I realized something.

They weren't worried about me. Hell, they didn't even know I existed. Yet here I am spending precious time and energy trying to figure out what their magic trick was to book so many gigs.

Then I was reminded of something my mentor Freddie Hendricks would always tell us back in high school, *"They got theirs. You betta get yours."*

I come from a great stock of actors. I am personally connected to hundreds of actors who had the pleasure to study under the tutelage of Freddie. To this day, when we see each other, we joke about his famous phrase. We joke because we never forgot it. It's what helped us perform around the world, create our own projects, win awards, perform on Broadway and network television.

"They got theirs. You betta get yours."

That finally clicked for me and made me realize that I am my own competition. The moment I stayed in my lane and focused on my race, things became so clear.

Instead of searching for clues on how other actors were succeeding, I began to search within myself. I searched for my strengths and weaknesses. I discovered that I had all the tools I needed to succeed. I just need to cultivate them and find ways to push myself.

The funny thing about focusing on your competition is that your mind will begin to tell you lies. Your inner critic will trick you into believing that you are not good enough. Sometimes the talent or beauty of another individual can make us think we are not up to par. That is the farthest thing from the truth.

There is only one YOU.

You can never be duplicated, only imitated.

There will never be a repeat of you in this form.

What is for you, is for you and no one else.

We are all in different seasons of our career. You may be comparing yourself to another actor who has been in the game twice as long as you. They paid more dues than you yet you feel entitled to all the success that they are currently achieving. You have no idea what they've been through. You have no idea what sacrifices they may have made. You haven't walked a mile in their shoes, nor have they walked a mile in yours.

It's human nature to think the grass is greener in someone else's yard. Your grass could be just as green if you took the time to water it.

The same is with your acting career.

The key to becoming a booking magnet is to focus on the star of your show... YOU.

What do YOU need to work on?

How can YOU improve?

How can YOU impress yourself?

How can YOU make yourself proud?

How can YOU beat your previous achievements?

When you stop worrying about your perceived competition and stop concerning yourself with the opinions of other people, you will amaze yourself at what you can accomplish.

You'll also realize that you have much more time on your hands.

Fear of Not Having Enough

We are abundant. We come from an abundant source. There is more than enough for everyone. What's for you is for you and no one can interfere with that. Period.

There's just one problem.

You don't always believe this.

You see, the fear of not having enough is a close cousin to fear of competition. You're so worried about what other actors are doing, why they are booking more and who they slept with rather than focusing on your own expansion and growth. It is the reason why you get so annoyed when you find out they've booked another gig and you haven't. Instead of celebrating them and their success, you send over vibes of jealousy and envy.

"They took my job. That role was supposed to be mine! I killed that audition!" Sounds familiar?

Somewhere along the line, you adopted a mindset of lack. You fell for the *okie doke* that there was not enough to go around. If an actor books a job you were interested in and also being considered for, guess what happens next? You begin to feel like they took something from you personally. They took food from your mouth. So the next time you hear about a role that you actually know would be perfect for your acting buddy, you keep it to yourself. GOD forbid they steal this role from you too.

This is a lie.

For a moment, I want you to envision yourself on a beach. The beach represents the entertainment industry. Each particle of sand represents an opportunity (television shows, movies, theatre, commercials, voice-overs, industrials, print jobs, dubbing, music videos, producing, directing, crew work, etc.)

You're still at the beach, and you have a large bucket. It's your personal bucket. All of a sudden you look around and you see millions of other people who also have their own bucket in their hands. On the count of three, you are all allowed to fill up your bucket with sand. I mean, fill it ALL the way up!

One, two, THREE!

Everyone fills their buckets to the brim with sand! There's sand OVERFLOWING from everyone's bucket including yours.

Guess what? You look around the beach and what is there still a ton of?

You guessed right. Sand. There's still more sand particles that are humanly impossible to count. There is more than enough, yet you were not cheated in the least bit, were you? You got to fill your bucket up as did everyone else.

I love this metaphor as it relates to our industry. I want you to keep this vision in mind the next time you feel like you need to hoard an opportunity from another actor.

Remember this fact: What is for YOU cannot be taken by ANYONE else. Your sand is yours and yours alone.

You must release your mindset of lack. There is more than enough to go around. My abundant mindset and approach to living is the reason I became the #1 Life and Career Coach for Actors. I give away information daily! I share everything with my audience. When I do live streams or YouTube videos, I always tell my audience that the secrets I am sharing are the actual strategies I have personally used to achieve success.

I honestly get a little upset when I think about all the years I spent fumbling and confused when I was surrounded by actor friends who could have given me some guidance along the way. It's all good though. I made a vow not to keep secrets because I believe they are not mine to keep.

I am aware that I am a magnet. You are a magnet. What we think about we bring about. The energy we put out towards other people comes back to us tenfold. I don't know about you, but I only want goodness flowing my way. When you begin operating your life and career at the highest frequency of love and abundance, you will experience a miraculous change in your outlook of life.

Your success and shine cannot take away the success and shine of another actor (and vice versa.) You asking more from GOD/ universe does not then deny someone else of their blessings. Ask away! Expect as much as you desire. There are no rations.

> "People with a scarcity mentality tend to see everything in terms of win-lose. There is only so much; and if someone else has it, that means there will be less for me. The more principle-centered we become, the more we develop an abundance mentality, the more we are genuinely happy for the success, well-being, achievements, recognition, and good fortune of other people. We believe their success adds to... rather detracts from... our lives."

> — *Stephen R. Covey*

Fear of Time Running Out

"If you haven't made it by the age of 25, then you might as well give it up."

If you're anything like me, you've heard someone, somewhere, spout this foolishness to actors.

We've decided to embark on a journey into an industry that praises the young. So it's only natural that we have issues with getting older. We hear actors and directors talking about how someone is past their prime or that an actor is now stuck in mom or dad roles.

Fear of time running out is what keeps people running to the plastic surgeon (I have no issue with it... I'm just sayin'...). It keeps actors on an unrealistic pursuit of staying young when it is not humanly possible. Just as in real life, you can't stay young forever.

Somewhere along the line, we've bought into Hollywood's notion that we can't be successful past the age of 30.

I'm always reminded of Morgan Freeman who really didn't start to get his film career popping until his big break when he was 50 years old. You know how the rest of his story goes.

I'm also reminded (and inspired) by the icon, Cicely Tyson, who at the time of this book being written is 94 years old and still going strong as a television and film actress.

I mentioned these two actors as a tiny example that IT IS NOT TOO LATE FOR YOU.

Many of the actors in my Hollywood Bound Actors online community are attracted to my teachings because I instill a ray of hope in their lives. For a lot of them, becoming an actor was a pipedream they long forgot about. After binging my YouTube videos and participating in my online classes and VIP retreats, they begin to realize that maybe there's still hope. They soon begin to take more classes, and my clients who really do the "work" end up booking more jobs.

In my experience, I've worked more over the age of 35 than I ever did before. When you are an actor in your early twenties, there just aren't as many juicy roles. You're a college kid, the sidekick or best friend. The big roles are so few and far between and highly coveted. Then by mid-twenties, you can experience what I did by being too young to be a parent or too old to be a student. You're kind of left in the messy middle.

I share this with you so that you understand that more is possible. There will always be a need for you at any age because television and film represent real life. We need babies, toddlers, teenagers, college students, aunts, uncles, moms, dads, siblings, grandparents, and everything in between!

I also personally believe that many actors give up long before they ever see their "big break." This should be good news for you because you plan on sticking around and not giving up on your dream. Your years of training and experience will help you stand out from the crowd.

If you are trying to break into this industry as a late bloomer now that you're done raising your kids or if you are just starting over, I want you to be encouraged also.

There is a need for you. As an actor, it's not all about what school you went to or what degree you have. If you have talent, you will work. If you take classes, get coaching and DO THE WORK, you can have a thriving career in this next chapter of your life.

Let no one tell you differently.

> "The most beautiful thing is that despite the shallow life we sometimes succumb to - the soul has no timeline and it knows what it wants and will yearn within until it seeks the journey."
>
> — *Malebo Sephodi*

By now you've surely recognized what's been keeping you stuck. One or more of the seven fears explained has been brought to light. So naturally, I know what you're probably thinking; *"Ok. So what now? How do I overcome these fears?"*

I've got you. I want you to take action.

I've created an acronym to teach you how to demolish these fears.

Here is my A.C.T.I.O.N. process:

A - **Acknowledge** that FEAR is always coming along for the ride. Don't let it shock you. Expect to run into fear when you are headed toward a greater destiny.

C - **Clarify** your WHY on a daily basis. When you remember WHY you are pursuing this career, and your WHY is strong enough, you won't let anything get in the way of your dreams.

T - **Trust** that you are good enough. Trust that you are worthy of every opportunity that presents itself to you.

I - **Ignite** your passion daily. Find a way to devote daily attention to your craft. It can be through writing, improv, reading, researching or visioning.

O - **Only** give time and attention to the thoughts, people, ideas, and things that uplift you and make you feel good.

N - **Never** forget that you are perfectly made. This industry may not know what to do with you at this moment in time, but there is nothing wrong with you.

Pushing past these fears is not an overnight process, but once you are armed with tools to succeed, you can't lose.

In part two of this book, I'm going to teach you how to *get magnetized*. This transformation is essential to your success as an actor.

You ready? Let's go!

Part Two

GET MAGNETIZED

What is a Booking Magnet?

It was 2017. My husband Garland and I had just moved back to Los Angeles from Atlanta, GA so that I could fully pursue my acting dreams. I quickly got settled and began booking high profile gigs. I felt as if I was on a role and I wanted to tap into what I was doing specifically to attract these roles.

I've been a student of the law of attraction since 2010. I began to study it during a dark time when I was going through my personal crisis. I searched for books and teachings that could help me understand why certain things were happening in my life. This work carried me through then, and it still does today.

What I understood when I moved back to LA was that I had to create the career I wanted. I knew that I had to speak life into my dreams daily. I had to take the time to visualize what I wanted to manifest in my life. Positive self-talk is essential for me and my daily success.

In case you are not familiar with the law of attraction, it is the belief that by focusing on positive or negative thoughts, a person brings positive or negative experiences into his or her life. As actors, we can often focus on the worst case scenario when it comes to auditions, bookings or our potential. You do, however, have a choice. I'm not saying it's always easy, but it is possible to become aware of your thoughts so that you do not constantly bring more negativity into your life.

I'm also a student of quantum physics (the study of the building blocks of the universe.) As humans, we are made of tissue and organs. They are made up of cells. Cells are made of molecules and molecules are made of atoms. I know, I'm taking you back to science class so bear with me. Atoms are made of subatomic particles. These particles are energy. So to break it down, YOU are energy. We all are. Everything is energy.

Whether you fully understand it or believe in science, it is a fact. We are energy, and we all put out vibrations. Some of us like to call it *vibe* for short.

Have you ever heard yourself say, *"I like her vibe?"*

What you are really expressing is the fact that you like the energy that this person is putting out in the world. It feels good to you.

We naturally want to be around people and do things that flow with our personal vibe. Everyone in your circle was drawn to you by the vibe you put. You attracted them to your life. So the kind of things you have been putting out will explain why certain people bring positive or negative energy to your life.

I've mentioned all of this to explain why I coined the term *Booking Magnet.* As I saw more auditions and bookings flowing into my life, I understood that I wanted to experience more of that daily. Since I understand that I am energy and that what I focus on expands (whether positive or negative), I decided to focus only on the positive. By calling myself a Booking Magnet, I see myself as a magnet with volts of energy in search of amazing experiences! I know that I'm great at what I do and I desire to attract more bookings, auditions, and amazing relationships into my life.

So, instead of doubting myself, I spoke life into myself. I still do it daily. If I don't, who will?

I am a booking magnet.
I am a booking magnet.
I am a booking magnet.

Even when you have zero bookings or no auditions, I want to invite you to speak this sentence to yourself over, and over and over again until it becomes your reality.

Whether you believe it or not, you are a magnet. If you don't like what you see around you, change your vibration. Make a new decision about what you desire to experience in your life. Don't be fooled by what you see right now. Give your attention to the positive and you will be amazed at how your life and career can change.

I am a booking magnet.
I am a booking magnet.
I am a booking magnet.

Who Is Your Veronica?

Now that you understand the power of the law of attraction and the benefits of speaking life into your dreams, it is inevitable that your inner critic is going to jump into the front seat of your brain.

Our inner critic can go by many names; ego, our limited self, the devil, etc.

Whatever you want to call it, we all have an inner critic. This is the voice that pops up in your brain that tells you your ideas are stupid. It tells you that you will never make it as an actor. This voice creates all the fears we learned about in part one of this book.

The problem that comes up for us is that we often confuse this voice with our own actual voice.

We hear the voice yelling loudly with all of these concerns. This voice is truly trying to protect us. It thinks that if it can talk you out of trying something new, stepping outside of your comfort zone or expressing a great idea, then you will be safe.

Wrong. No, thank you. I don't want that kind of protection. This protection is what keeps too many of us playing small and safe. This voice tells us that we suck as actors and that we might as well give up.

When teaching this to my clients, I remind them that your personal vibration is akin to a light switch. It is either on or off. Positive or negative. Either you are in the driver's seat, or your inner critic is.

This is why I want you to try something a bit unorthodox. I want you to give your inner critic a name. Yes, a name. I want you to pick a name that describes the personality of this nagging voice.

Okay, I understand that you may have just read the sentence above and might be looking at this book with the same perplexed look my students give me during my live workshops. Yes, I know it seems weird. Just trust me.

Here's why I want you to try this; it is imperative that you fully understand that the voice you are hearing is not YOUR voice. Yes, it may sound like you in your head, but it is not you.

By giving it a name, you are acknowledging that the thoughts coming up are not what you truly believe.

You... are not calling yourself stupid.
You... are not telling yourself your idea is dumb.
You... are not telling yourself that you're too old, too fat, or ugly.
You... are not talking yourself out of going to that audition that could change your career.

It is not you.

So who is it?

My students often hear me talking about Veronica. That's the name I gave my inner critic. She is a nasty woman, let me tell you! She's mean and cruel and always manages to pop up when I have a great idea. The beauty of me giving her a name, and understanding what it feels like when she is around is what gives me power. When she is around, my "light switch" is off. The energy is negative. She has nothing empowering to say. Once I realize this, she and I have a conversation. Yes, I talk to myself. Don't act like you don't. We're actors for goodness sake!

"Veronica, have several seats," I say. *"Not today girl. This is a good idea, and I am going to see it through even though I'm nervous. I got this. I don't need you to protect me today girl. Got it?"*

These are real conversations by the way. To tell you the truth, Veronica tried to talk me out of writing this book. I refused to listen to her because I knew that my purpose had to be greater than my fears. I knew actors all over the world needed this book the same way I did. So thankfully, she did not win.

I know this seems weird, but it works.

Here's the deal. Your fear is always going to come along for the ride. The misconception is that our fear will someday dissipate and we will become fearless in the pursuit of our dreams. That is never going to happen. Once we accept that, we can learn to feel the *fear and do it anyway.* You can do what I like to call **play scared.**

I want you to get this. Your inner critic only comes around and opens his/her big mouth when you've got something good going on. If they get really loud, know that your idea must be amazing!

If you play small, stay in your (un)comfort zone and don't risk anything, your inner critic won't have anything to say. You're safe. The challenge begins when you step into your destiny with full force and positivity.

Don't be distracted or fooled by what will come up. It is not YOU.

So, what shall we name your inner critic?

May I Take Your Order?

I'm about to ask you a really hard question. It will seem basic as hell, but I dare you to answer it in five seconds or less.

What do you want?

More specifically, what do you want from your life and career?

See? I told you it was a hard question.

I've been a coach in one way or another for many years now, and this question is the one that stumps my clients the most. Why? It's because we are so used to letting life happen to us rather than being crystal clear about what we desire to experience.

Here's the hard truth...

If you are not specific about what you want to do, have or be, you will not fully experience life on your terms.

Your life is like the Cheesecake Factory® menu.

In case you've never been there, allow me to explain. The Cheesecake Factory® is a national restaurant chain that boasts a wide selection of food as well as their signature desserts. The only issue you will have as a customer is deciding on what you want to order. Why? Their menu is like fifty pages long! I'm exaggerating (a little.) There are so many options to choose from. It's kind of funny actually.

Imagine you go to the Cheesecake Factory®, and the server asks what you'd like to order for dinner. You tell them that it doesn't matter or you don't answer them at all. You're totally fine with letting them pick your item because you're too busy, distracted or just not in the mood to make a decision. About 20 minutes later, the server arrives with your food. There's just one problem - you don't like what they delivered. You eat it anyway because, hey, you didn't make a choice. With each bite, your stomach turns a bit. The food is not going down well at all, but you muster through. You go home and feel ill the rest of the day, and you decide to sleep it off and start fresh tomorrow.

The next day, you head back to the Cheesecake Factory® (or any restaurant for that matter), and you do the same thing. You allow the server to order for you and the story repeats itself. Even though you hate it, you go to a new restaurant every day expecting a different result when in fact you are experiencing your very own Groundhog Day.

This is how many of us live our lives.

When you read the story above, what did you think? Were you wondering why this person didn't just take the time to read the menu and decide what they really wanted to eat? If they didn't like the food when it arrived, why not send it back and order something else? Why choose to do the same thing every day at a new restaurant and expect a different result?

The answer is simple. Many of us don't realize that we have a choice. We can create our experiences. If we get something we don't like, we can put in a new request.

Your life is like the Cheesecake Factory® menu. You've got options — many of them. So I will ask you again...

What do YOU want?

In order to live your life by design, it is imperative that you start answering that question on a daily basis. Remember, the universe is abundant! There's more than enough to go around for everyone. It is impossible for you to ask for too much. There's just one catch. You must put your order in with the universe.

What kind of gigs do you want to book?
Who would you like to meet?
Where would you like to travel?
What roles do you want to portray?
What food would you like to eat?

The best way to come up with these answers is to take quiet time every day and allow yourself to daydream. I know our grade school teachers used to tell us to *"Snap out of it! Stop daydreaming."* Well now, dear actor, you have permission.

Take time every single day to envision the life you want to

live. There are no wrong answers, but trust and believe, if you don't create the life you want to live, someone else will. Many actors are living the lives their parents, family or friends want them to live. Not you. Not now. No more.

Let's agree that yesterday was the last day you allowed life to happen to you. You are now on a journey of self-exploration. You now know that you can put your order in with the universe and co-create your existence here on earth.

Don't worry about HOW your desires will come to pass. All you need to do is hold steadfast to the vision in your mind's eye. See it. Believe it. Plan it. Achieve it. You will be surprised at how events will align in your life once you decide what you want.

I love this quote I often see online:

> "Speak what you seek until you see what you said."

> — *Anonymous*

What Do You Expect?

I'll never forget the day I was at Hartsfield Jackson International Airport in Atlanta, GA. I had a 6:30 AM flight to Los Angeles for an in-person audition. I, along with other customers found it odd that TSA had not opened the security checkpoint gates at 5:30 AM. The line was getting longer and longer, and surely we would all need at least an hour to get through.

Would a bunch of us miss our flights due to no fault of our own?

Clearly, we were all thinking this, but most of us just contemplated it silently, trusting that the TSA would finish their morning staff meeting and let us through.

About 15 minutes later, the security checkpoint finally opened. Though there were hundreds of customers needing to get screened, I was not worried. I had a deep knowing that I would make my flight.

Such was not the case for a frantic older woman a few feet behind me. She began yelling at employees about how she was about to miss her flight due to their negligence. Her voice grew louder as her arms flailed. *"I'm going to miss my flight! I'm going to miss my flight! You have to let me through!"* Her wild behavior caught the eye of an employee who ended up letting her jump the line ahead of the rest of us who also had the same flight time.

The whole scene was a straight comedy for me. Why? I realized that this woman had such low expectations for the day. Yes, the TSA opened the security checkpoint late. Yes, there were hundreds of people ahead of me. (This was before TSA PreCheck was a thing.) I was not bothered or panicked because while I stood in line, I saw how I wanted the day to work itself out. As I stood there, I visualized myself going through the checkpoint with ease, stopping to grab a snack, using the restroom, boarding the plane, putting my carry-on luggage in the overhead compartment and then finally sitting down next to a lovely person who did not snore or have a crying newborn. That's where my mind was. That was my expectation of the day.

I must admit, I chuckled to myself as my zone was called to board and the woman who made such a fuss in the checkpoint area was one person ahead of me. One person! She put herself through such stress and anxiety, and for what? We both made it on the plane but had two very different experiences.

Since then, I've always used that day to remind me to keep my expectations high. Not just for traveling, but for my life and career.

So, I will ask YOU…

What do you EXPECT from your life?

What do you EXPECT from your career?

What do you EXPECT from today?

I want to invite you to raise your expectations.

One of the most powerful tools we have as actors is our imagination. It's how we bring characters to life. It's how we draw an audience into the world we've created. If there's one thing we know how to use, it's our imagination. The only problem is, outside of performing, we usually use our imaginations to create and rehearse the worst case scenarios that can happen in our lives.

If we have a big audition, we imagine ourselves screwing it up.

If we have an agent meeting, we imagine the team not wanting to sign us.

If we're just getting started in acting, we imagine that we won't be accepted because we're too old or too green.

If we think about marketing ourselves to industry power players, we imagine that we will get blackballed and never work again.

The list goes on and on. Do you see the issue with this?

Remember, your imagination is a powerful tool. I want you to use it for good.

I want to challenge you to tap into your inner five-year-old who used imagination fully, with no judgment of fear of failure. The child inside of you knows what it's like to play pretend and be fully invested in the outcome.

I want to challenge you to look at your life day by day and expect the best. If you must rehearse a scenario, rehearse the best version of it.

What we naturally do as humans is to think about what we do not want to happen. So we spend time pondering the worst thing that can happen not realizing the law of attraction is always at work. If you think negatively, negative shows up. If you think positively, positive shows up. The law knows no difference. It is only tuned into what you are thinking about. What you think about, you bring about. What you resist, persists.

This is why it is more beneficial to ask yourself, *"What DO I want to happen? What outcome do I desire?"*

Do you see how this is an empowering question? Now you get to use your imagination for good by coming up with the best case scenario. When we ask ourselves questions, our brain is hard-wired to come up with an answer. It's just science. I want you to try it. I also want to warn you that your inner critic will get loud at this point. Why? Because it's trying to protect you from all those sweet, aspiring thoughts you're coming up with. Don't listen to the voice!

When you raise your expectations, you will change your life. Give it a try.

> "Powerful people ask powerful questions. Why? Because questions steer focus and in life, we only get what we focus on."
>
> — *Trevor Otts, Founder BlackCEO*

Part Three

HOW TO AUDITION LIKE A BOOKING MAGNET

You've Already Won

Now that we've laid the foundation for a winning mindset, we get to have some fun. You finally get the call or more likely, an email, telling you that you have an audition. It may be an in-person appointment or a self-tape request. Either way, it's a real opportunity with your name on it. It's time to celebrate because you've already won.

Yes, seriously. Celebrate.

I know what you're probably thinking. *"Christine, it's just an audition, not a booking."*

That, my dear actor, is where you are wrong. It is a booking.

Never forget these instructions:

Book the Audition.
Book the Room.
Book the Role.

Confused? Allow me to explain my thought process.

Do you realize that there are thousands upon thousands of actors across the world who desire to be an actor just like you? Right now, there is a person who looks similar to you and has a similar vibe. There are so many actors at home praying for a call... any call that would allow them to show off their talents. So, when you get picked from the thousands of headshot submissions and agency pitches, you are already winning. You have won. Never forget that. Think back to the time when you looked forward to the day you could audition for a television show or a movie. It felt like a faraway dream, right? When you finally got requested those first few times, it felt surreal, right? Yes, you may have been nervous or excited, but deep down you knew you were on the right track.

When you approach your career with an attitude of gratitude and stay in search of ways to celebrate, it will help you create a career that you are proud of.

So I intentionally say, *"I booked an audition"* because that is a fact. I celebrate that. Many actors did not even hear about this opportunity. It happens to me all the time. Some of my girlfriends will go out for a show that never came across my lap. Remember, every role is not for everybody. So make sure you celebrate your industry friends as well.

Your next celebration is when you book the room. That simply means that you felt good about the work you did and you made a fan. I will reiterate, only one actor can book a role. Production has to make a choice. They are not always easy choices. Sometimes the reason you don't book a gig can come down to the tiniest details that have nothing to do with you. Hold onto this fact by setting the intention to go to your audition (or submit your self-tape) and win over the room. When you book the room, you will know it. You will leave with a smile on your face because no matter the outcome, you know you gave it your all. That is all we can ask of ourselves... to do our very best and to make ourselves proud. The only person I am competing with is myself. The same is true for you.

If the cards align, the next thing you can be grateful for is when you book the role. This is clearly a no brainer. You did it! Not only did you get selected to audition amidst thousands of actors worldwide, but you became the chosen one for this particular project. Celebrate that with your whole heart and know that one booking does not automatically lead to the next. You must continue to show up in a way that best represents who you are as a professional actor.

Do you see how shifting your paradigm around these repetitive moments can bring more gratitude and joy into your life? When you operate your career with this mindset, you can't lose. It will also guard you against becoming jaded and spewing negativity to those around you. If more actors adopted this attitude of gratitude, our industry would change drastically.

Prep For Success

I see so many actors sabotage their opportunities due to lack of preparation. It is what separates the amateurs from the pros. Professional, working actors understand the need for having a process that helps them win. Amateurs are fine with winging it and hoping for the best. Which type of actor are you?

Have you ever found yourself waiting until the last minute to study for an audition?

Have you waited until the very last minute to submit a self-tape?

Have you ever left an audition knowing that it was sub-par because you knew you needed coaching, but for some reason, you decided to skip it?

Have you ever felt frazzled in the audition room because you didn't have enough time to settle down before your name was called?

We have all been there at some point in our careers. I want to share my personal audition prep strategies with you. I still go down this list for every audition. Seriously. I share this list often as a free gift to my community, and I get tons of questions asking if this stuff really works. Yes. I am a booking magnet because this process has helped me build confidence over the years. When your confidence shines through, there is no stopping you!

Here is my **Get Booked Checklist:**

1. Get a good night's sleep. - Getting rest is crucial to audition success. You want to feel refreshed so you can put your best foot forward.

2. Wake up early. - The day of an audition is not the day to sleep in. Allow yourself extra time in the morning to ease into the day. You want to approach your day with a relaxed, positive mental state.

3. Drink something warm. - Your voice is an instrument. Having a warm cup of water or a cup of tea will allow your vocal cords to wake up gently.

4. Stretch. - Your body, like your voice, is an instrument. Do some gentle stretches to let the blood flow through your body.

5. Inhale/Exhale 5 times slowly. - Deep breaths not only relax you, but they help to improve blood flow, increase energy, reduce inflammation, detoxify the body and more!

6. Listen to your "Get Booked! Playlist." - Create a playlist on your cell phone with the songs that pump you up. Pick songs that make you feel confident and alive, sexy and unstoppable. Listen to your playlist in the car and the waiting room for ultimate impact.

7. Print your sides for the ride to the audition. - I love to read my lines at the red light on the way to an audition. If you live in a city where you use public transportation, even better! This is a great time to get in a bit more studying.

8. Pack a pair of headphones. - You will want your headphones to listen to your affirmations or your playlist in the waiting room. You don't want to disturb anyone.

9. Pack at least 4 headshots/resumes. - It never hurts to bring extra, current headshots and resumes with you. Be sure that they are already stapled together and ready to be given away if asked. You never know, there may be another casting office in the building. Why not do a drop-off?

10. Arrive 30 minutes early. - Give yourself time to find parking, use the restroom and get settled in the waiting room. If you are rushed, everyone will feel it.

11. Sign in and settle down. - Sign in no earlier than 15 minutes before your appointment time and go over your lines or listen to your playlist or affirmations.

12. Inhale/Exhale 5 times slowly. - Allow your brain to relax with deep breathing. Trust me, this will help to calm any nerves that are creeping in.

13. Visualize your audition. - See yourself audition and envision the best possible outcome.

14. Enter the room in character. - The moment you step foot in the audition room, you should be in character. Even during small talk, refrain from popping out of yourself too much. Keep the energy you had in the waiting room.

15. Find your mark. - Locate the area on the ground where you need to stand/sit.

16. Scope out the room. - Take in your environment with a quick scan.

17. Locate the camera and the reader. - Take notice of where the camera is and who is reading with you. In the event you rehearsed it differently, this allows you to readjust your plan quickly.

18. Decide on your focal points. - Find spots on the wall that you can use for additional focal points besides your reader if needed.

19. Work the camera, not the room. - Remember, at the end of the day, all casting will do is send your video to producers for review. Focus less on impressing casting in person with your personality, and focus more on your on-camera performance.

20. Listen to redirects, ask questions if necessary and take your time. - Be fluid and be present. If you have questions, ask.

21. Slate in character. - Don't lose character when asked to slate. Stay in the zone and say your name and height as the character you just portrayed. Don't ruin the fantasy!

22. Say thank you. - Before leaving the room, be sure to thank the casting director for taking the time to see you.

23. Leave a thank you card. - Write a quick note to the person who was in the room and leave it at the front desk with the receptionist. If you don't know their name, ask!

24. Listen to your "Get Booked! Playlist." - On the way home, be sure to listen to your playlist as a celebration of a job well done.

25. Express gratitude for the opportunity to do what you love! - This is the most important part. Not everyone has the same opportunities that you have. Express gratitude that you were able to do something that you loved today.

Waiting Room Warfare

Definition

noun

The use of propaganda, threats, and other psychological techniques to mislead, intimidate, demoralize, or otherwise influence the thinking or behavior of another actor in the audition waiting room.

Pretty dramatic chapter title 'eh? Well, when you work in a town full of actors, that is the only way to describe what happens in some audition waiting rooms.

I'm fully aware that many of you are in smaller markets or in a market where they mainly self-tape. Trust me though, there will be a time when you have a callback or a producer's session, and you will be forced to sit in the same room only inches away from your perceived competition.

Times have changed. If you are reading this book, you are working in a time where technology has really changed the game. I'm about to date myself here, but back in the day, self-tapes were not a thing. I remember living in Atlanta, GA and having to drive to New Orleans, Louisiana for 8 hours so that I could spend two minutes in the audition room. I would then turn right back around for another eight-hour drive home. I'm still grateful for my road trip crew and my best friend, Kail, who took most of those trips with me. So, by the time self-taping was created, it made it so much easier for casting directors to find talent, and it made it so much easier for us actors.

Though I am spoiled by self-taping in the comfort of my home studio, I must be honest and tell you that I still relish in-person appointments. I like meeting casting directors, producers and showrunners face to face. It allows them to feel my energy that does not always fully translate from watching me on camera. There's only one downside to in-person appointments... dealing with other actors.

Don't get me wrong. I love to network and schmooze with the best of them. However, every actor has their own method or process for auditioning, and I want you to be prepared so that it doesn't throw you off your game once your name is called.

For many years, I have experienced what I like to call "Waiting Room Warfare." I coined this term to describe some of the antics that I've experienced over the years as groups of actors wait their turn to audition. Allow me to explain further. You've heard of the phrase *psychological warfare,* right? Well, waiting room warfare is a real thing, and I want to give you some tips on how to protect yourself from it.

The fact of the matter is, we all want to book the role. Unfortunately, not all actors play fair. Instead of just showing up, being quiet, and focusing on the job at hand, some actors feel like they need to mess with the competition. Get inside their head. If they can get you to screw up your audition, that's one less person standing in the way of their booking.

If you are in the Broadway circuit, this looks like actors, singers or dancers going above and beyond to warm up their voices or bodies in close proximity to you. They may talk loudly to other actors about how they just worked with the director or how hard the dance combination is going to be. Some performers who lack confidence will sniff out the weak, the green, the nervous; they come for blood.

If you are on the television and film circuit, waiting room warfare shows up a bit differently. You may be sitting in your chair trying to focus, and all of a sudden a **"Chatty Cathy"** will show up and start talking your head off about nonsense. This person doesn't even need you to respond. They just want you to stop studying your lines and get distracted. That way, when your name is called, you are kind of frazzled. Score! To be fair, some Chatty Cathy's are just extremely nervous about their own audition, so this is how they cope. Do you see how this still comes down to lack of confidence?

The next character that may show up to throw you off your game is the **"DIVA."** This can be someone of any gender by the way. This actor makes it a point to talk loudly while they rattle off their most recent credits to the entire waiting room. *"I just flew in from London..." "This casting office loves me...." "OMG, I've had so many auditions this week. I just tested for nine pilots last week!"* You get the point right? Their goal is to make you feel inferior... like maybe you should just pack up your things and go because this other actor is clearly the chosen one. The tactics of the Diva can be convincing, especially if they are a celebrity or someone you've seen on television for years.

I also want you to beware of the actors who are spending too much time before their audition catching up. It's inevitable that you will run into your friends at some auditions. Heck, the more you audition in person, the more actor friends you will make. However, it's important that you establish a communication code that respects both parties. There will always be at least two actors who are talking loudly about random stuff. It can be extremely distracting.

The last character I want to make you aware of is the **"Bitch."** Yup. That is not a typo, and again, does not relate to any one gender. This actor will stare you down as soon as you walk in the room. They will size you up without blinking an eye as if you stole their money. It will confuse you. Just remember, the look of disgust on their face or their rolling eyes have nothing to do with you and everything to do with them.

No matter which character pops up in your audition waiting room *(there are more, by the way, these are just the usual suspects)* just know that many of these actors are suffering from a crisis of confidence. They are also stuck in a lack mentality.

When you know that you've taken the time to study and prepare your audition, you will naturally feel confident. It's natural for nerves or excitement to creep in once you've arrived at your audition, but at the core, you feel good about the work you are about to do. Not everyone feels that way when they arrive. Maybe they got the audition late, and they're not off book. Perhaps they are in a bad mood. It could be that the actor is just not a good auditioner. Whatever the case may be, don't let their insecurities or issues affect your audition.

Some of the characters I mentioned do not lack confidence. They lack an abundant mindset. These actors are talented, and they know it. They've got their looks, charm, and an impressive resume to stand on. Unfortunately, they look at everyone else as a threat. In their minds, they believe that there is not enough to go around. They feel like they have to hoard opportunities and knowledge. So, if they can throw off your focus or intimidate you, they have won at protecting what they perceive to be theirs. As we discussed in part two of this book, we live in an abundant universe. This entertainment industry is vast and filled with opportunities.

If I can impart any words of wisdom to you, it is this; don't fall for the story that you have to tear down another actor for you to rise. You can shine at the same time another actor shines. You can have a successful audition without sabotaging anyone else.

Do not let anyone psych you out while you are in the waiting room. I don't care if you see your favorite celebrity auditioning for the same role as you, do not throw in the towel. Mark my words; YOU ARE AT THE RIGHT PLACE AT THE RIGHT TIME.

You are exactly where you should be. You made it in the room. You got invited when thousands of other actors did not. Do not squander this moment because you got star-struck or because someone got in your head. You will regret it.

Instead, breathe. Put your headphones on. Listen to your lines and visualize yourself winning.

Focus on your *real* competition. You.

Tell Your Story

You've been studying for two days. Your audition is in three hours, and you feel ready. You know your lines, you analyzed your script, and your outfit truly reflects the essence of your character. You feel ready and energized. More than that, you feel prepared. Confident even. You head on over to the audition and arrive thirty minutes early (because that's what professionals do.) You sign in and walk into the waiting room, and then it happens.

Your stomach starts to cramp up, and your heart rate increases dramatically.

You make a run to the bathroom just to be safe. Your palms are sweaty, and you don't know why. You were perfectly fine at home.

You get it together and head back to the waiting room. Two minutes later, your name is called. You enter the room, and you feel totally off your game. You fumble your lines and begin apologizing to the casting director. You finally make it through the entire scene, but you are not happy with it. Then you hear the dreaded *"Thank you."*

You leave the room and head back to your car defeated. You're pissed because those damn nerves took over your body again. The real you actually never stepped foot in that audition. Your nervous representative did. You go home and wonder if that casting office will ever call you again. The next audition you get forces you to replay this scenario over and over again, and you wonder if you even have what it takes to book another role. Instead of learning from the experience, it now haunts you.

Any of this sound familiar?

You are not alone, trust me.

I've been in the business for over twenty-five years, and nerves are always bound to creep up. It's a natural human reaction, so I'm not about to tell you that you can rid your nerves forever. I do, however, want to share one crucial tip that can drastically change how you approach auditions. This one paradigm shift will help your confidence skyrocket and will help you book more roles.

Turn your nerves into excitement.

Instead of saying, *"I'm so nervous!"* Replace that sentence with, *"I am so excited!!!"*

Try it now. It feels totally different, yet almost the same. At its core, nerves are just balls of energy and excitement flowing through your body. This excitement can cause all kinds of random, and sometimes embarrassing things to happen to your body. The fact that you have this reaction shows that you care about what is about to happen. If you didn't want to audition or if you hated the role, you would be so chill.

Your brain is processing all the fun things that will happen as a result of you auditioning. You get to meet the casting director. If you book it, you get to work on a cool new show with celebrities. You will get screen time. This role could have a huge impact on your career!

This is a lot to think about. No wonder you're excited! It's perfectly normal.

Remember this; never let ANYONE prevent you from telling your story.

When we let our nerves take over and sabotage our auditions, it prevents us from telling the story of the character we've spent so much time creating. I personally believe that it is my job to bring a character's truth to light. It is my job to show up and be excellent because no one can tell this story better than me.

When you walk in a room, let your nerves take over, fumble lines and apologize excessively, you give your power away.

Stop giving your power away!

You are capable of amazing things. Do not let anyone tell you otherwise. Casting directors and producers like to work with actors who are confident and who can bring fresh ideas to the table. You are co-creators with the singular goal of creating a great finished product. They want you to win. They want you to be THE ONE.

From the moment you walk into the audition room or submit a self-tape, casting is secretly praying that you bring something special to the table. They want to look at you and think, *"We've found our lead. This is the actor we should present to the network."*

Never let anyone prevent you from telling your story.

I don't care if the traffic was horrible or if public transportation was late. I don't care if the other actors in the waiting room are acting like fools. I don't care if the casting director looks disinterested. If I get an appointment and I show up, I am telling my story. Period. What happens next is out of my hands. I can't control if I get a callback or if I book the role. The only thing I can control is me and my performance.

I learned this powerful lesson after my own series of horrible auditions. The story that opened this chapter happened to me more times than I care to admit.

I will leave you with a mantra that has helped me book tons of roles throughout my acting career:

I AM powerful and talented, and I have a story to tell.

Try saying this to yourself right after they call your name. It will change your swagger and the way you walk into the audition room.

You can thank me later.

See. Hear. Feel.

Becoming a booking magnet will require more than just luck. It will require you to tap into your senses on many levels. Most actors don't realize they are already using these techniques. Unfortunately, they are using it to their detriment.

I am a huge advocate of using the V.A.K. technique in the way that some athletes are trained to use it.

You may be familiar with the acronym: V (visual), A (auditory), and K (kinesthetic.) The V.A.K. learning style uses these three main sensory receivers and is a tool typically used by teachers to determine the best way a student likes to learn.

Though this is the basic definition of the technique, some coaches urge their team to use these three senses to help prepare them to become champions of their sport.

I was really drawn to this concept when I researched it years ago while life-coaching women. I never let this concept go and have since begun to use it for my acting career as well as with my acting clients.

Here's how you can use the V.A.K. technique to have a killer audition;

Step One:

Sit in a quiet place (this may even be used in the actual audition waiting room) and **Visualize** yourself in the audition room. You walk in, you are greeted with welcoming smiles. You see yourself in the room standing on your mark. You seem to be at ease... confident even. You hit every beat, and you are in tune with the reader. You nail the audition and see yourself leaving the room and walking to your car. You did that!

Another way I like to use visualization is to see myself not only in the audition room or at a producer's session, but actually on set. Many actors do not do this work. They limit their imagination to the casting office — not me, and not you.

Visualize yourself pulling into crew parking and stepping into your trailer. Your contract is on the table waiting for your signature. Your costume is hanging up. You then get escorted to hair and makeup, and then you're invited to rehearsal with the cast and director. You have an amazing read through. You and the director have a good vibe going. When it's time to shoot, it feels effortless. You are confident and prepared. Once you wrap, the director tells you what a great job you did. You sign out and head back home. You take a hot shower and have a snack while relaxing on the couch. You head to bed soon after knowing that you had an amazing day.

Do you see how powerful this visualization is? Do you see how detailed I get with what I desire to experience?

Step Two:

Using everything you created in your mind's eye with the visualization technique in step one, use the **Auditory** technique to create the sound around you. As you walk in the audition room, what do you hear? You hear the casting director say, *"Hi. Thanks for coming in. How are you?"* Once your read through is done, you hear someone in the room whisper, *"Wow. That was amazing. Really. Thank you."* You leave feeling confident. As you walk back to your car, you hear the birds chirping and the wind blowing. The next morning, your heart flutters with excitement when your agent calls to tell you that you have a callback with the producers! Your agent sounded more excited than usual because this role might recur and will look amazing on your new demo reel. You find out a few days later that you actually booked the role. While you are on set, the director yells, *"Action!"* and you almost shed a tear. You've arrived, and it feels amazing.

Do you see how we're going to another level by hearing positive sounds?

Step Three:

Alright. We're still building upon steps one and two. Okay? Let's go back to the same visualization of walking into the audition room. Begin to think about how your body will feel. The use of the **Kinesthetic** method will allow you to be in tune to yourself so that your nerves won't take over. When you get out of your car, your pulse is racing a bit, but that's just excitement. You know you are right for this role, and it feels good. When you get to the waiting room, you are calm. You are taking long, deep breaths. You are the epitome of zen. As you walk into the audition room, you feel like you are floating (in a good way.) You're chill and confident. You are definitely someone these casting directors want to work with. When you see your agent's phone number appear on your phone the next morning, your heart races with excitement. You feel pride and joy after you hang up from the good news. When you arrive on set (because of course, you booked the role), you feel a sense of overwhelming gratitude flowing through your veins. By the time you get home from a long day of fun shooting, you're tired... in a good way.

This, my dear actor, is how I prep for roles. Sure, just like you, I don't book every role I audition for. No one does. However, this preparation makes me feel good, and that's all that matters.

You don't have to perform each of these steps separately. I've used this technique so many times, and I am used to combining all the senses during one visualization session. It's actually hard for me to see and not feel, or see without hearing. They all go together for me.

The fact of the matter is, you are using the V.A.K. technique already whether you realize it or not. You're just using it to rehearse the worst case scenario. How does that help you? Wouldn't you rather feel good stepping into an audition? Be intentional about how you desire to feel before, during, and after each appointment. It will make a world of difference in your approach and your booking ratio.

With mental rehearsal, our minds and bodies become trained to actually perform the skill imagined. So allow yourself to imagine the best possible outcome.

Remember, our imagination is our most powerful tool as actors. Use it for good.

Part Four

BACK TO ONE

In case you haven't figured it out already, this book is all about mastering your mindset. When you change the way you look at life, your life will change.

We've covered a lot so far, and I've probably struck a nerve with you here and there. You might not be happy about it, but you are aware now that someone finally sees you. It's easy to get lost in a sea of never-ending to-do lists, audition tips, and marketing strategies. At the end of the day, even if you technically know everything you could do to further your career, sometimes you just don't feel like it. Sometimes you feel uninspired. Lack of auditions, feedback, rejection, stress, and the constant hamster wheel of this industry can make you want to throw in the towel. I get it because I've been there. I've been there... often.

When you are feeling this way, go back to one.

As film and television actors, we are used to hearing the 1st AD shout, *"Back to one!"* We know what this means. It means that you are about to do that scene over again and you need to go back to your first position so you can start over.

Sometimes we need to go *"back to one"* in our daily lives. For me, this means going back to your WHY.

Your WHY is the reason you decided to become an actor in the first place. It's what motivates you to show up for this demanding career day after day, year after year. What naturally happens to us is we forget that acting should be fun and become frustrated and jaded with our career when we don't feel it is unfolding the way we originally envisioned. We see friends and associates making moves, becoming famous household names and we wonder, why not me? Why not now? These thoughts and feelings can destroy you.

I've seen actors who have let the entertainment industry destroy their confidence, drive, and self-worth. So much weight gets put on *"making it"* that you can lose sight of the real reason you started.

Go back to one. Go back to WHY.

Why did you decide to become an actor?

Take a moment to think about this question. You'll notice that there's power in the word, DECIDE. No one made you choose this career. You decided to take on the judgment, frustration, excitement, and stress of this career. Why?

If you're anything like me, acting has been a lifelong dream. I enjoyed talking to myself (and my dolls) while playing pretend as a child. I loved to dance and record my voice to create characters. I performed for free for so many years because it was never about the paycheck. Of course, I make a living as an actor now, but let's be clear, that hasn't been the case for most of my adult life.

When I ask members of my Hollywood Bound Actors Facebook group why they became an actor, I get responses like:

Acting is my ministry.

Acting is my purpose.

Acting fuels me.

Acting gives me freedom.

There is never any mention of money or fame. Naturally, many of us aspire to walk the red carpet and win awards, but that is not at the foundation of our WHY.

Acting should be fun! You have to remember that. If auditioning brings you stress and overwhelming anxiety, you should stop now. Please. Get a full-time job doing something else. You could even work behind the scenes. You may find that being a part of the crew is better suited for you.

I don't share this in jest. I've met many casting directors and acting coaches who flat out told me that being an actor was just too hard. They couldn't deal with the endless pressure and rejection. It did not make them happy. So they found something else to do in the entertainment industry that brought them joy.

Why did you decide to become an actor?

I want you to write your answer down in a journal or on a piece of paper that you will not lose. You can even email the answer to yourself.

When you are experiencing a day (or month) of frustration, and you think you want to quit, I want you to find your answer. Read it aloud. If you still agree with your WHY, take a nap and start fresh the next day. If you are no longer in agreement with your WHY, I would like you to look within and discover what you are passionate about now.

As we grow, our passions change. Our circumstances change. Marriage, children, divorce, disease, and death can force us to take a look at our lives and wonder if we are truly living.

Whose life are you living? Are you living the life you envisioned or someone else's?

Go back to one. Go back to why.

You are a booking magnet. Believe it to be so, and so it shall be.

An Invitation:
BECOME A BOOKING MAGNET

Join The Booking Magnet Academy and take your acting career to the next level.

I want to help you take everything you've learned from this book about mindset and put it into action. Now that you've been armed with the tools to master the way you think about acting and auditions, it's time for you to start using next level strategies to book more work.

The Booking Magnet Academy is the #1 virtual training center for actors who want to book starring roles in film and television over, and over, and over again.

This monthly membership will give you access to my methodology that has helped my bookings skyrocket! You will learn how to master your M.A.M.A.: Mindset, Acting Technique, Marketing, and Audition Technique. You will learn how to uplevel in all these areas, and your career will thank you for it!

I know you're going to love it. I hope to see you on the inside!

www.bookingmagnetacademy.com

About The Author

Christine Horn is an award-winning actress and singer who has performed in feature films, primetime television, and on Broadway. She is a Life and Career Coach for Actors and the creator of the online hit show, Actors Daily Bread, where she pulls back the curtain of her own career to teach actors around the world how she cracked the code on consistently getting booked.

She is the founder of the Booking Magnet Academy, the #1 virtual training center for actors who want to master strategies to book starring roles in film and television shows consistently. Christine has helped hundreds of actors learn how to take control of their career and turn themselves into master marketers and booking magnets. Her signature 4-step methodology has helped her clients increase their pins/holds/callbacks/producer sessions in less than 90 days.

As an actress, Christine's experiences and accomplishments are diverse and vast giving her a special ability to relate to all audiences. With over 20 years of professional experience, she has graced stages across the U.S. with Disney's "The Lion King" and has performed for President George W. Bush at the White House.

Her extensive theatre background led her to the silver screen where she has appeared alongside a plethora of Hollywood A-Listers... Adam Sandler, Drew Barrymore, Charlie Hunnam, Chiwetel Ejiofor, Jon Voight, Tyler Perry, Columbus Short and Allison Janney, just to name a few.

Christine has starred in some of your favorite television shows, some of which include The Good Doctor, Timeless, American Crime Story, NCIS, S.W.A.T., Ray Donovan, Powerless, Good Girls, Legion, Greenleaf, The Originals, Complications, Tyler Perry's The Haves and the Have Not's and Reckless.

When she's not performing or coaching actors in Los Angeles, Christine enjoys spending quality time with her husband, Garland, her dog Prince, and her turtle, Superstar.

Connect With Christine Online

Official Website
www.christinehorn.com

Hollywood Bound Actors
www.hollywoodboundactors.com

Instagram
www.instagram.com/actresschristinehorn

Facebook
www.facebook.com/actresschristinehorn

Twitter
www.twitter.com/hornchristine

LinkedIn
www.linkedin.com/in/actresschristinehorn

Made in the USA
Las Vegas, NV
09 May 2021

22692601R00066